TS MOST ADVANCED,

NO MATTER WHAT
PEOPLE SAY,
THIS BOOK IS
NOT
A DIARY.

DUDE DIARY 3.0

Write stuff
Draw Random Things
Destroy if needed
AGAIN!

WRITTEN & DESIGNED BY MICKEY & CHERYL GILL

...and i helped

UNDER THE CONTROL OF LITTLE ORANGE MEN FROM MARS

FINE print
PUBLISHING

Fine Print Publishing Company
P.O. Box 916401
Longwood, Florida 32971-6401

ISBN 978-189295162-5

2 3 5 7 9 10 8 6 4 1

thedudebook.com

PROPERTY OF:

IF YOU BREAK INTO
THIS BOOK, I AM TRAINED
TO CRAWL ONTO YOUR
FACE, UP YOUR NOSE,
AND ULTIMATELY,
INTO YOUR BRAIN.
ONCE THERE, I WILL HAVE
FULL ACCESS TO YOUR
CEREBRAL CORTEX.

You're part of a super elite group of international dudes. The survival of humanity rests on your shoulders.

(It's pretty important stuff. You might have to wear a tie.)

Dude, is there a fire hydrant nearby?

Something reeks. It must taste good.

You have no time for diaries. You're developing secret plans and keeping them under lock and key. Design an intergalactic space program,

keep a log of suspicious smells, rule an island empire, & recruit members for a secret society. You have a lot on your plate.

Proceed to secured entry.

FOR ENTRY, YOU MUST SCAN YOUR HAND HERE

AND LEAVE YOUR THUMBPRINT BELOW

USING A #2 PENCIL, COMPLETELY FILL IN THIS BOX. PRESS YOUR THUMB ON IT.

LEAVE YOUR THUMBPRINT.

SECURITY

TRACE YOUR HAND ABOVE

IS YOUR BRAIN BIG ENOUGH TO ANSWER THESE DIFFICULT QUESTIONS?

HOW TALL ARE YOU? 4 feet

HOW TALL IS YOUR HAIR? Halfin

LENGTH OF YOUR BIG TOE?

landa half
holes

DIRT UNDER YOUR TOENAILS?

yes

WHAT MAKES YOU BURP?

Food

WHAT ARE YOU AN EXPERT AT?

Sports!

WHAT GIVES YOU EXPLOSIVE GAS?

Gas

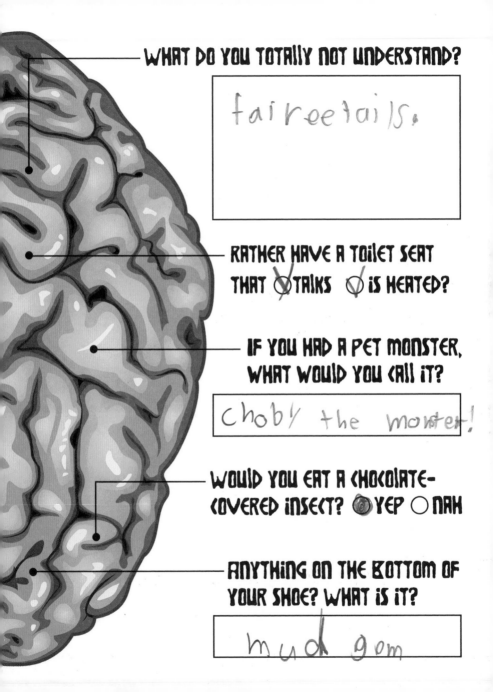

WHAT DO YOU TOTALLY NOT UNDERSTAND?

faireetails.

RATHER HAVE A TOILET SEAT
THAT ~~TALKS~~ ✓ IS HEATED?

IF YOU HAD A PET MONSTER,
WHAT WOULD YOU CALL IT?

choby the monster!

WOULD YOU EAT A CHOCOLATE-
COVERED INSECT? ● YEP ○ NAH

ANYTHING ON THE BOTTOM OF
YOUR SHOE? WHAT IS IT?

mud gom

SMELLS FISHY

LIST ALL THE STOMACH-CHURNING STUFF YOU COME ACROSS.

my brotherfrfats. my moms fats.

my fats.   my poops.

my brothers fish.
              poops.
roal fish.

WHICH IS THE NASTIEST? WHY?

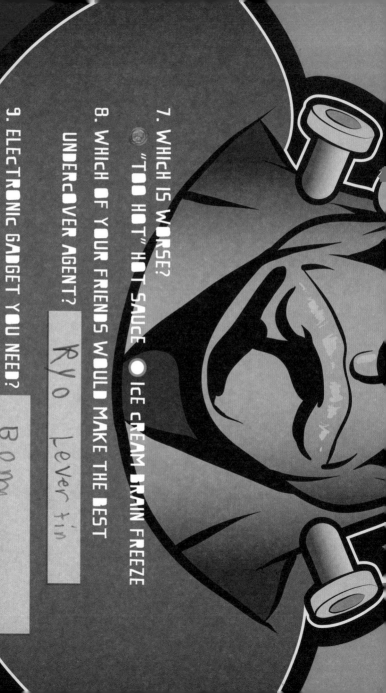

7. WHICH IS WORSE?
   ⊙ "TOO HOT" HOT SAUCE ⊙ ICE CREAM BRAIN FREEZE

8. WHICH OF YOUR FRIENDS WOULD MAKE THE BEST
   UNDERCOVER AGENT? Ryo Lever tin

9. ELECTRONIC GADGET YOU NEED? Bom

10. I WOULD RATHER EAT DIRT THAN poop!

1. WHO'S SCARIER? ○ ② HEADLESS HORSEMAN ○ FRANKENSTEIN

2. WHICH IS BETTER? ○ SUBSTITUTE TEACHER ○ NO HOMEWORK PASS

3. RATHER BE THE
   ○ HULK
   ○ THING?

4. RATHER SHOOT
   ○ SNOW FROM YOUR MOUTH
   ○ FIRE FROM YOUR BUTT?

5. COOLEST THING YOU'VE EVER FOUND?
   a pea of medle

6. FAVORITE NUMBER?
   6
   WHY? Because I like it

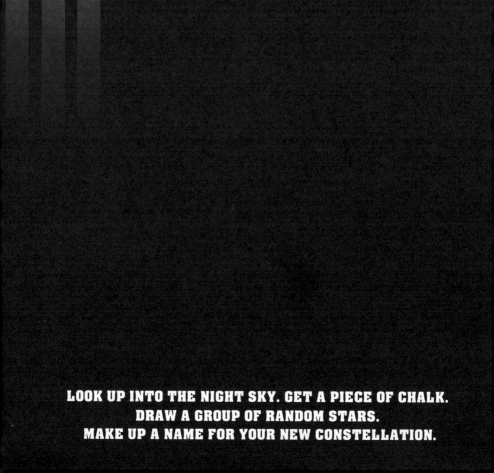

LOOK UP INTO THE NIGHT SKY. GET A PIECE OF CHALK.
DRAW A GROUP OF RANDOM STARS.
MAKE UP A NAME FOR YOUR NEW CONSTELLATION.

WHATEVER YOU DO,
DO NOT
WRITE OR DRAW
ON THIS PAGE.
OR ELSE.

BECOME A M

 1. Draw your face really big in the large square below.

2. Then cut out the 9 small squares.

3. Mix up the small squares and tape or glue them to the grid in this frame.

YOU BE THE

WHO WOULD WIN? WHY?

GODZILLA **VS** KING KONG ___Godzilla___

NINJA **VS** SAMURAI ___Samurai___

A LEPRECHAUN **VS** THE TOOTH FAIRY ___Leprechaun___

DARTH VADER **VS** LORD VOLDEMORT ___Lord Voldemort___

THE JOKER **VS** LEX LUTHOR ___Lex Luthor___

YOUR LIFE IS  AN AWESOME VIDEO GAME

NAME THE GAME

S Wave ?

YOU MUST HAVE A CHALLENGE.
A REALLY HARD MATH PROBLEM, CHORE, OR SOMETHING LIKE THAT.
DRAW OR DESCRIBE THE ENEMY.

YOU'LL NEED A CREATURE SIDEKICK TO FOLLOW YOU AROUND AND HELP OUT. DRAW OR DESCRIBE.

FINALLY, YOU NEED A GAME HERO NAME.

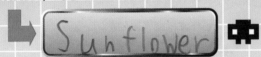

Sunflower

DRAW OR DESCRIBE WHAT YOU LOOK LIKE, YOUR BATTLE ARMOR, AND HOW YOU TAKE ON AN ENEMY!

MAKE YOUR TRIP TO SCHOOL WAY COOL!

TRICK OUT A SCHOOL BUS, CAR, BIKE, SKATEBOARD, OR YOUR SHOES & BACKPACK IF YOU WALK.

SHARE YOUR INCREDIBLE PLANS HERE.

I fart to shcool.

If your friends were dogs, what kind would they be?

Friend   **Dog**

_____   _____

_____   _____

_____   _____

_____   _____

_____   _____

_____   _____

_____   _____

_____   _____

the intergalactic

Your initials

SPACE PROGRAM

You're heading up a new space exploration project.
Name the spacecraft and plan the mission.

Spacecraft Name...................................

Draw name on the spacecraft ➜

Destinations.............................
(Where your crew will fly to)

....

Mission...............................
(What your crew will do)

....

....

....

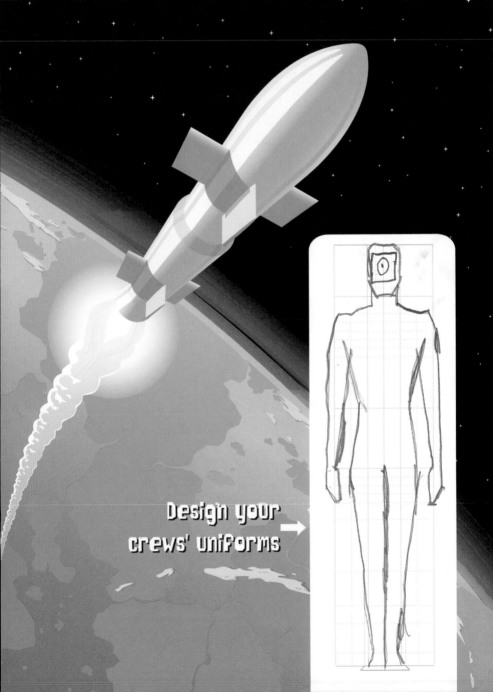

Design your
crews' uniforms →

All the things that really annoy me

Ben

Ticks really tick me off.

MOUTH MIX-INS

COMBINE YOUR FAVORITE SNACKS IN YOUR YAPPER AND NAME YOUR NEW SNACK COMBOS!

SNACK NAME		SNACK NAME		NEW SNACK NAME
_____	+	_____	=	_____
_____	+	_____	=	_____
_____	+	_____	=	_____
_____	+	_____	=	_____

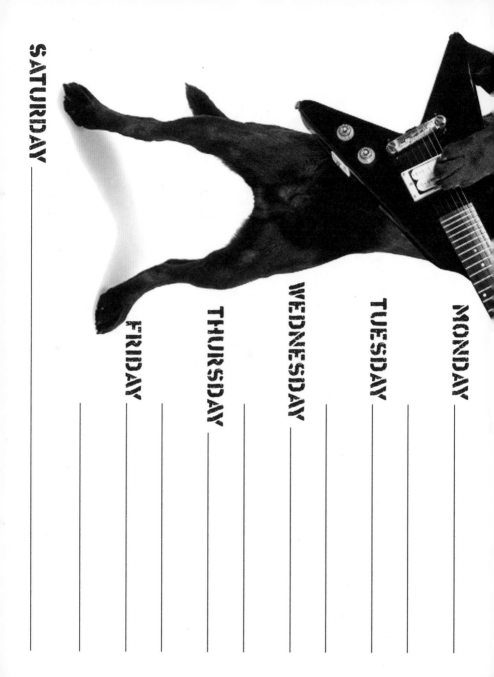

SATURDAY _____

FRIDAY _____

THURSDAY _____

WEDNESDAY _____

TUESDAY _____

MONDAY _____

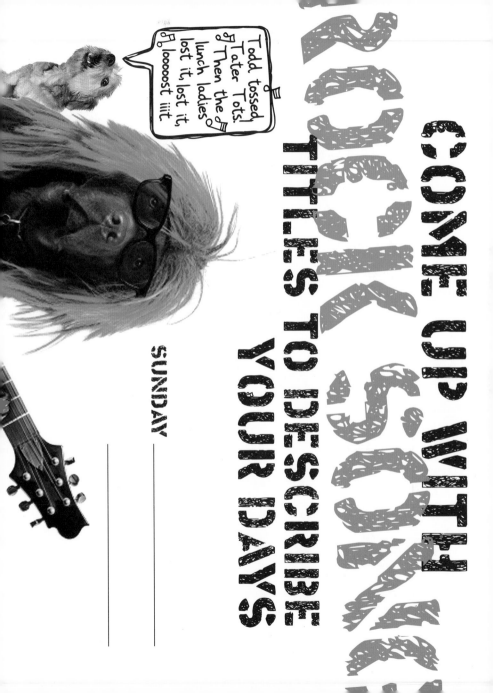

THIS IS YOUR ISLAND. YOU'R

Island name Gabwensoltinlard.

Your official title
- ○ King
- ○ Master
- ○ Sir

National food

National pastime
(Favorite thing
to do on the island)

Animals that live here

_____   _____

_____   _____

WN PERSONAL
IN CHARGE

Yes!

Design your
island flag

Draw your
home

Add islanders'
homes

Who or what is forbidden on your island nation?

_____

IT'S A REMOTE CONTROL TO RULE YOUR WORLD!

FILL IN ALL THE BUTTONS WITH STUFF YOU WANT TO BE IN CHARGE OF.

What if I could get my dog Mr. Stinky to toot on command? Awesome!

THE BOYS' BATHROOM

at school
would be way better if it ...

1. _____

2. _____

3. _____

4. _____

5. _____

YOU'VE HAD TO CLEAN UP?

_ _ _ _ _ _ _ _ _ _ _ _

7. EVER WEAR
CAMOUFLAGE?
◉ YES
○ NO

9. RATHER HAVE
AWESOME RECTUS
ABDOMINUS
◉
INCREDIBLE BICEPS?
○

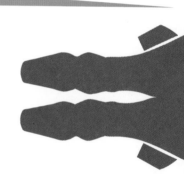

YOU DID THAT
YOU WERE TOLD
NOT TO DO?

bad things.
_ _ _ _ _ _ _ _ _ _ _ _

8. PAINTBALL GUN
◉
SUPER SOAKER?
○

10. BACON?
◉ YES!
○ YUCK

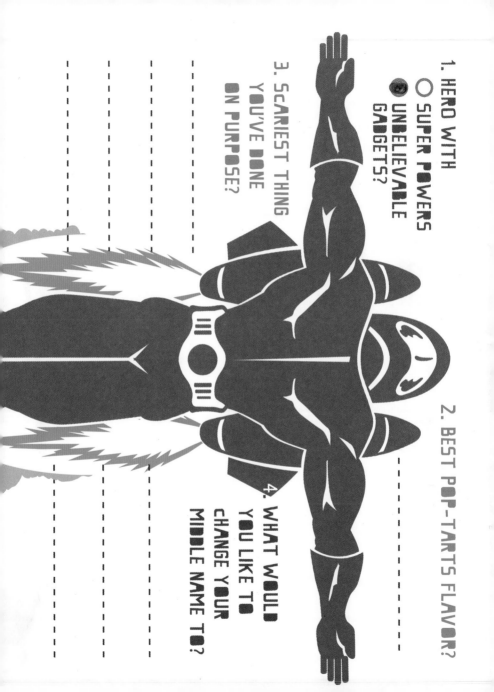

1. HERO WITH
   ○ SUPER POWERS
   ● UNBELIEVABLE GADGETS?

2. BEST POP-TARTS FLAVOR?

3. SCARIEST THING YOU'VE DONE ON PURPOSE?

4. WHAT WOULD YOU LIKE TO CHANGE YOUR MIDDLE NAME TO?

Finish this thought.

I WANT MORE.

I want more ants for my ant farm.

Really? Cuz I wan more humans for...

Finish this thought.

I NEED LESS ...

Whoa dude, I'm outta here.

Fresh Sushi

THE ULTIMATE JOB

If you had to get a job, what would you like to do? Why?

I wanna run a sushi place for otters!

ss sspick me or I'll sssqueeze the ssstu...

WOULD YOU RATHER...

- ☑ **Have a 2-headed snake as a pet**
- ☑ **Be the official taste tester at your favorite restaurant**
- ☑ **Trade places with a movie star for a week**
- ☑ **Become a character in your fave video game any time**
- ☑ **Drive the Batmobile for one day**

who

1. has green eyes? _yes_

2. is Left-handed? _yes_

3. can't stand rock music? _yes_

4. was born in a different country?
   yes

5. can speak a different Language?
   yes

6. thinks he/she has seen a u.f.o.? _yes_

7. makes straight A's? _yes_

8. is always Late? _yes_

9. gets out of bed on the right side?
   _no_

10. Likes to eat sardines? _yes_

FINISH THIS STORY.

I SAT DOWN TO DO MY HOMEWORK WHEN I SAW A U.F.O. FULL OF MONKEYS.

I didn't do my hom
wk in school and
went in it. The
monkeys did ther

homework for me.
I had a party at
the ship and ate
candy and played
baseball there. I went
to the blue jays game.
I went to a foot-
ball Game. I Went to
a hockey Stanley cup
finals Game.

... AND THAT'S WHY I FORGOT TO DO MY HOMEWORK.
THE END.

MAKE A MAP OF YOUR CLASS

Like you are looking down at it from the ceiling.

Only Spiderman can do that.

Draw desks and write each student's name on each desk. Place all the extras - trash can, flag, funny things on your teacher's desk. Whatev.

Start a frozen banana stand.

Turn my backyard into a jungle gym.

I would run for my life!

Also get a gun!

Play video Games?

SO YOU'RE THE HOST OF YOUR OWN TV SHOW.

What's it all about?
Is it a reality show, game show, or what?
Do you invite guests to appear on it?
Who would be your co-host? Share all the deets.

game show, hosted
by a booger?

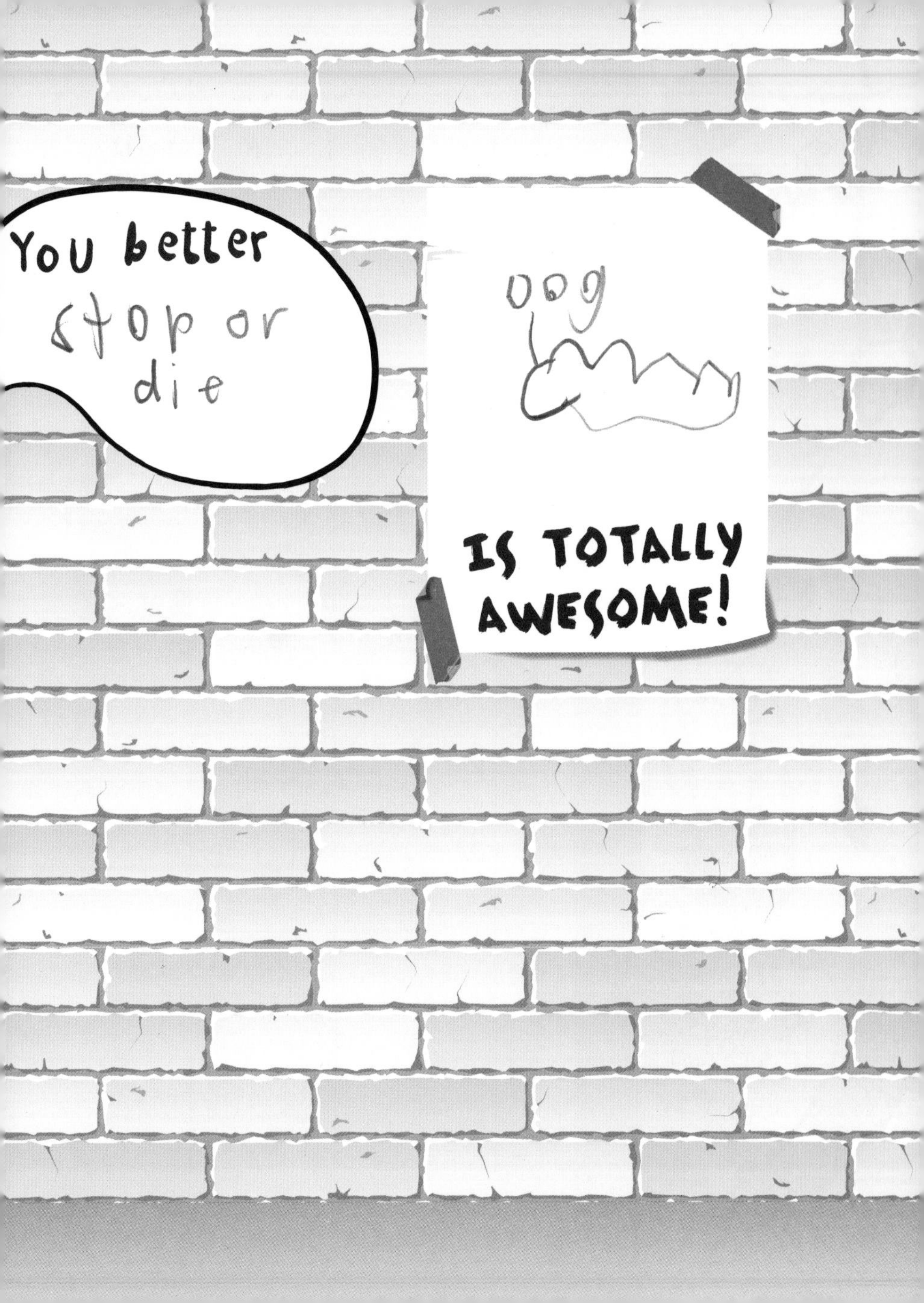
You better stop or die
oog
IS TOTALLY AWESOME!

MY KID rocks

sports.

(Name of school)

AT

...is the best
arm farter!

MAKE YOUR OWN

BUMPER STICKER

FOR THE FAMILY

FILL IT IN WITH WHAT YOU'RE THE BEST AT,
ARE KNOWN FOR, OR SOMETHING YOU DID.

Dude, how old
is your dad's car?

PLAN THE MOST OUTRAGEOUS, OVER-THE-TOP, EPICTACULAR BIRTHDAY EVER IN THE HISTORY OF BIRTHDAYDOM!!!

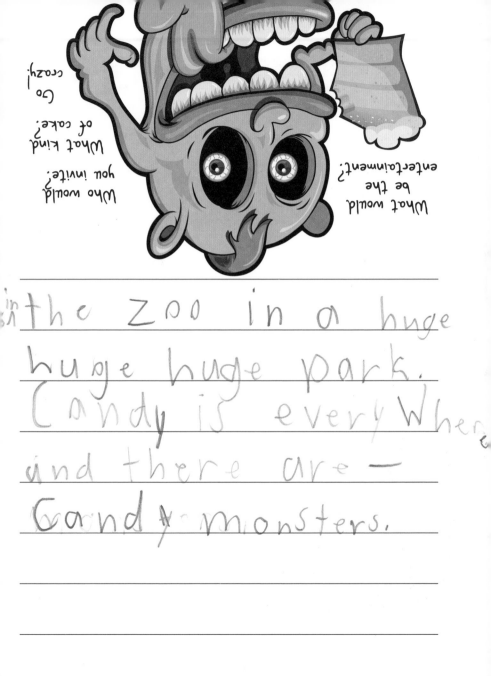

Who would
you invite!

What kind
of cake?

Go
crazy!

What would
be the
entertainment?

in the zoo in a huge
huge huge park.
Candy is every Whe
and there are —
Candy monsters.

DUDE, THA[T

(That's kinda like a list)

Keep a tally of all unacceptable behavior.

(That's like burping, farting, underarm farting, etc.)

Name

Ben

Ben

Ben

Ben

Ben

Ben

Ben

Ben

oops

S SO RUDE!

our friends' & family's
hen choose a winner.

What they did

farts!
farts!
farts!
farts!
poops!
pees!
farts!
pees!

BRAAP!

AND THE
WINNER
IS

Ben

7. ● MONSTER
   ○ MONSTER TRUCK?

8. ● SKATEBOARD
   ○ CASTERBOARD
   ○ OTHER _ _ _ _ _ _ _ _ _ _ ?

9. DO YOU HAVE FRECKLES?
   ● NO
   ● YES
   HOW MANY? 4,000,000,000

10. RATHER BE A CERTIFIED
    ○ GENIUS
    ● RACE CAR DRIVER?

1. CIRCLE ANY AREA THAT'S EVER BEEN HURT. IF YOUR BRO, SIS, OR SOME DUDE AT SCHOOL CAUSED IT, PUT THEIR NAME NEXT TO IT.

2. RATHER BE A
○ CYCLOPS
○ TRICLOPS?

3. WHAT'S GROSSER?
● GETTING HIT BY BIRD POOP
○ STEPPING IN DOG DOO

4. ● POCKET NINJA
○ BACKPACK TROLL?

5. FAVORITE KINDA DIP?
ketchup

6. FAVORITE FOOD TO DIP?

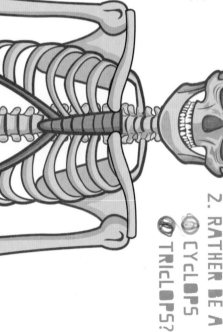

Put all the bad, rotten, or embarrassing things that happen to you in the path of Godzilla.

LOOK OUT A WINDOW

AND DRAW OR DESCRIBE THE SHAPES YOU SEE IN THE CLOUDS BELOW.

[DO NOT ATTEMPT THIS AT SCHOOL.]

GET YOUR HAND

Here's a place for all your things you don't like people touching. List, draw, or tape them down here.

I hate

KEEP OUT

OFF MY STUFF!

You person.

THIS IS YOUR
PERSONAL ASSISTANT. ⟶
WHAT CAN HE DO FOR YOU?

1. kill pepole!!!!!!!
2. kill popove
3. kill
4.
5.
6.
7.
8.
9.
10.

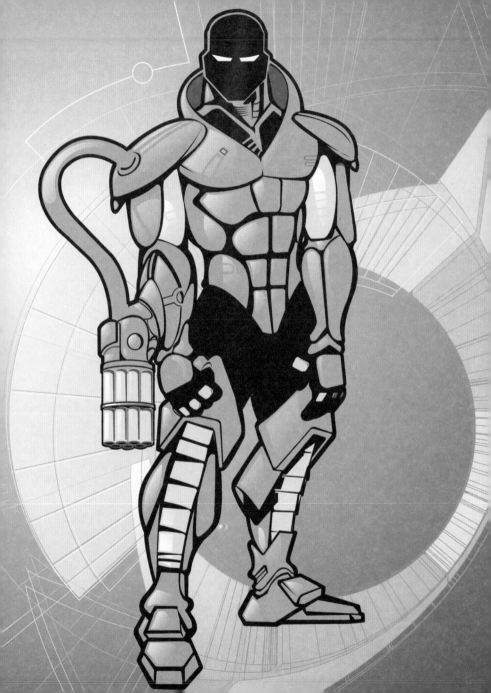

START YOUR OWN ➡

WHO WOULD YOU LIKE AS MEMBERS?
[FRIENDS, FAMILY, FAMOUS PEOPLE, SUPERHEROES, YOUR PET HAMSTER]
LIST NAMES AND TITLES NEXT TO NAMES.
[SECRETARY, TREASURER, PRESIDENT, FRENCH FRY GUY, ETC.]

```
┌─────────────────────────────┐
│                             │
│                             │
└─────────────────────────────┘
          YOUR NAME
```

NAME	TITLE	NAME	TITLE
Henry	thing	What?	What?
kal			
Skull			

MISSION [WHAT YOU MEET ABOUT] _____

SECRET
SOCIETY

NAME OF SECRET SOCIETY

SECRET SOCIETY PASSWORD

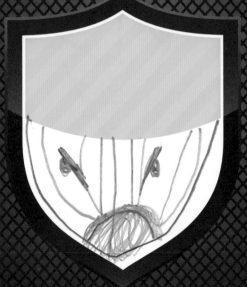

DESIGN YOUR SECRE SOCIETY CRI

DRAW YOUR SECRET HAND SIGNAL.

WHICH IS WORSE?

1. ☑ HAVING A BLACK BELT GRANNY WHO LIKES TO SPAR WITH YOUR FRIENDS
   ☑ TEACHER WITH AN EYE ON THE BACK OF HEAD

2. A WORLD WITHOUT ☑ HAMBURGERS ☑ HOT DOGS

3. A WEEK WITHOUT ☑ HANGING WITH FRIENDS ☑ GAMING

4. DISCOVERING ☐ ANCHOVIES IN YOUR FAVORITE DESSERT ☑ WORMS IN YOUR SPAGHETTI

5. A BUNCH OF ☑ DUDES WITH NO GIRLS IN SIGHT
   ☐ GIRLS WITH NO OTHER DUDES IN SIGHT

6. ☑ CAT WHO BLURTS OUT WHATEVER YOU'RE THINKING
   ☐ DOG WHO TELLS YOUR PARENTS EVERYTHING YOU DO

7. A WORLDWIDE SHORTAGE OF ☐ FRIES ☑ POTATO CHIPS

8. ☑ WIPING OUT FACE FIRST ☐ FALLING DOWN BACKWARDS

9. ☑ WARM SODA ☐ MELTED ICE CREAM

10. ☐ SMELLY BATHROOM ☑ SMELLY BATHROOM WITH SICKLY SWEET AIR FRESHENER

YOUR GANG OF

Brainstorm what to call them here.
Think of what they like to do, wear, or eat.
Use this info for their names.

[   ]

FRIENDS NEED some NICKNAMES

It doesn't matter if they already have nicknames.
You can come up with something better.

name of friend	ohmazing new nickname
~~k~~wak	Swag
sWak	the bag
thWak	fat Dog
tWak	SWock

WHO DO YOU COMPETE WITH –

FOR GRADES?
ATTENTION?
IN GAMING?
IN SPORTS?

(or anything else you can think of)

DOES IT BOTHER YOU? OR DO YOU LIKE IT?

me·

i LOVE a good competition

He makes me so mad

WHAT TIME WOULD YOU START?
WHAT WOULD YOU STUDY?
WHAT WOULD YOU HAVE FOR LUNCH?
WHAT WOULD YOU DO FOR P.E.?
(AND ANYTHING ELSE THAT WOULD MAKE MON.-FRI. WAY BETTER)

nevon have school?

DO YOU HAVE WHAT IT TAKES TO BE A DETECTIVE?

Find out. Take this challenge.

List everyone you talked to today.
Include any details you can remember -- what they
were wearing, carrying, & what they told you.

Name & deets

_____

_____

Name & deets

_____

_____

Name & deets

- -

- -

Name & deets

- -

- -

Name & deets

- -

- -

Name & deets

- -

- -

Name & deets

- -

- -

You're awesome, and you know it. But what if you could have a few added features, pushing the boundaries of awesomeacity?

Choose from the list of "extras" below. Describe or draw the upgraded you.

Australian accent

Bionic arm

Ice-dispensing mouth

Purple eyes

GPS-wired brain

Lie-detecting sunglasses

Popcorn popping backpack

Time-travel watch

Hair that ignites into flames

Off-the-chart IQ

Glass-shattering burps

Play guitar & drums at same time

Speak rat

Electronics-charging ears

Snake charmer

Sign in Martian

Grow dinosaur tail on command

Candy flavored earwax

Boom

$1 \div 1_{600} = 1$

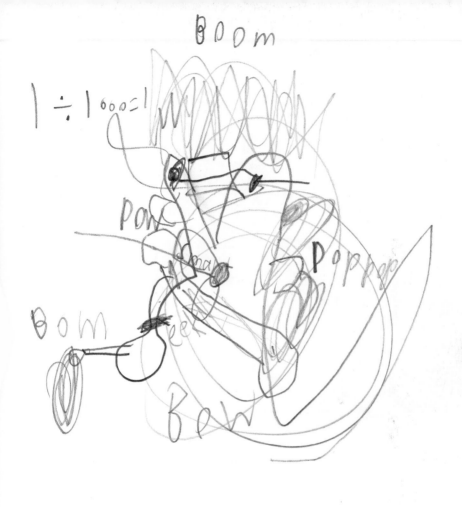

Pon

Poppop

Bom

Bew

Look around your house.
Find an object.
Make sure you don't
know what the object is
or what it's used for.

Sketch it.
Describe it **OR** stick a
picture of it

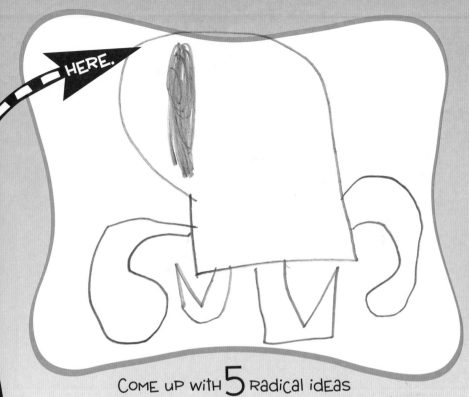

HERE.

COME UP WITH **5** RADICAL IDEAS
OF HOW YOU COULD USE THE OBJECT.

1.

2.

3.

4.

5.

YOU'RE ON THE HUNT

HUNT

FOR:

SOMETHING DIRTY & SMELLY _
What is it?

A KID NAMED JASON _
His signature

 A FOUND
PENNY Tape it here

SOMETHING BROKEN _
What is it?

A HOLE PUNCH _
Where did you find it?

AN OBJECT THAT STARTS WITH THE LETTER U

What is it?

AN OBJECT WITH 3 WHEELS

What is it?

SOMETHING THAT'S RUNNY, DRIPPY, OR OOZING

What is it?

AN ITEM IN YOUR ROOM THAT DOESN'T BELONG TO YOU

What is it?

A DEAD BUG

Tape it here

FOOD IN THE FRIDGE THAT'S REALLY GROSS

What is it?

You have discovered a NEW INSECT!
You must share your findings with the scientific world.

Is it ☐ annoying ☐ harmless ☐ deadly?

How does it "BUG" humans? _____

_____

_____

Where does it live? _____

_____

What does it eat? _____

_____

What does its poop look like? Draw

Sketch your buggy discovery here.

THIS IS A TOTALLY

GROSS GOBLIN

HE FEEDS ON FILTH IN DUDES' BEDROOMS.
WHAT COULD HE EAT IN YOUR ROOM?

[LOOK UNDER YOUR BED, IN THE CORNERS OF YOUR ROOM,
BOTTOM OF YOUR SHOES, AND IN YOUR TRASH.]

_____

_____

_____

_____

_____

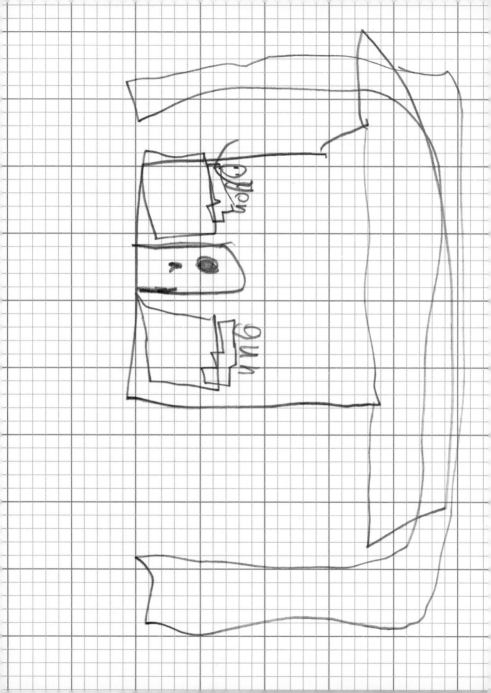

TURN YOUR HOME INTO A FORT

Draw a diagram of your house. Add an underground tunnel, a few cannons, a moat, or whatever you need for an indestructible fortress!

Write here

_____
_____
_____
_____
_____
_____
_____
_____
_____
_____
_____
_____
_____

NICE ONE!

_____

WHAT UP DOG?

Write here

AWESOME!
BACON IN 3D.

Hey, dog breath, over here!

BOO-YAH!

THIS IS REDUNKULOUS.

Write here

Yo poochie,
you smell great!

AWWWW YEAH!

GOTTA GET
OUT ARF HERE!

YEAH, WHATEVER.
GIMME YOUR
ANKLE!

Bro, need your
back scratched?

WHAT AM I DOIN' HERE?!

Write here

Hey mutt,
I need a ride!

LET'S MOTOR!

SORRY I
GOT YOUR
BOOK WET.

Write here

MAN UP AND GET YOUR HANDS ON
THE ENTIRE UNIVERSE OF BOOKS THAT
STARTED IT ALL -- DUDE, DUDE 2, AND
THE DUDE DIARIES.

CLICK ON WWW.THEDUDEBOOK.COM
FOR MORE CRAZY BRO STUFF!